Preface to Prenatal Charts

Charles A. Jayne

ISBN-10: 0-86690-620-7
ISBN-13: 978-0-86690-620-3

Cover Design: Jack Cipolla

Published by:
American Federation of Astrologers, Inc.
6535 S. Rural Road
Tempe, AZ 85283

www.astrologers.com

Printed in the United States of America

Contents

Preface   v

Introduction   vii

Chapter One, The Basis of an Arcane Astrology   1

Chapter Two, The Astrology of the Soul   25

Chapter Three, Procedure for Prenatal Charts   35

Chapter Four, The I Epoch of Inspiration and of Isis and the T Epoch of Ties and of Pluto   63

Appendix, Locality Shifts   71

Preface

This book, one of a series on arcane astrology, is an attempt to provide material in a branch of astrology which is the least authentic of all its divisions. It is hoped that whatever we can contribute will be studied and tested by our colleagues. For esoteric knowledge should eventually become widely known or exoteric.

It is a cardinal tenet of ours that each new level of more complex organization in the hierarchy of real Wholes reveals new and higher attributes of reality. A real cluster of stars is more significant than the same number of single stars. A real set of prenatal or postnatal charts in their interrelationships reveal more features of the higher attributes of Man than one can find in those charts singly. Thus, in *The Secret Doctrine*, Madame Blavatsky correlated galaxies with Atman, the seventh and highest principle in Man, whereas single stars correspond only to the fourth principle or Animal Soul.

A galaxy is comprised of billions of stars but is, in addition, not just a congeries but a genuinely integral entity. The failure to recognize this vital principle by astrologers is one reason why most of their work on esoteric astrology cannot be taken really seriously. In the work we did on Non-natal Epochs and their charts, Eleanor Hesseltine and I were aided by a great teacher without whose help we could not have discovered what we did. This book is dedicated to her.

Introduction

This book is divided into four chapters. Chapter One contains the new material that describes the whole system of cosmic centers and their related epochs. Chapter Two contains material on five of the seven prenatal epochs and their charts that take place during the year before birth. In addition there is material on one regular postnatal epoch, that of the Mars Epoch of Purpose and its chart. Chapter Four has material on the I and T charts. If one or more of these prenatal epochs occurred at a different locality than that of the natal epoch, be sure to look at the Appendix, where information is given on how to handle such cases.

I wish to acknowledge the help given to me by my wife in all of this work, for without her counsel and other vital forms of help, none of it would have been possible. These charts and their key planets open the door to a genuine arcane astrology of the Soul.

Charles A. Jayne

Chapter One

The Basis of an Arcane Astrology

A fter a lifetime spent in the study and practice of astrology, I have reached certain conclusions as to its basis. I
am not a member of the Theosophical Society but a theosophist at heart as I have been since I first learned about astrology from the librarian of the West Philadelphia.Theosophi-
cal Society in 1932. My teacher, Oris Baker, had been in
France. Oris was born the same month, day, and year as Dane
Rudhyar, the best-known of living astrologers. At one time I
was aided in my work by a great teacher whose teacher was
the same as Madame Blavatsky's. Nonetheless, I assume full
responsibility for trying to condense a vast subject. I find that
the basis of a genuine arcane astrology is in accord with Theosophy and the doctrine of the Ancient Wisdom in other
forms.

Astrology over many, many millennia has passed through
four major phases. The first one was mainly in the preliterate
period. During that time major and real groups of stars were

accented, but the zodiac was not in evidence. Chronology was lunar rather than solar, and the shift to a male (and solar) dominated society had not yet occurred.

During the second millennium B.C. the Sun and the Sun gods and sons of God became primary. The Sun and the plane of its apparent annual revolution, the ecliptic, became important as the zodiac, for which this plane is central, emerged.

By the time of the advent of the Christian Era and the Age of Pisces, the planets were increasingly important, although 1,100 stars were still used by the classical Arabic and Hellenic astrologers. They brought in the third phase. During the earlier second one, investigated in some depth by Cyril Fagan, the stars had been paramount and the fixed or sidereal zodiac was central. In the third phase the moving, or tropical, zodiac of the seasons came to the fore except in Asia. The whole trend was away from the timeless, remote, and vast to the kinetic, near, and relatively smaller (the planets) over the precession of the millennia.

In the West under the fourth and modern phase, the stars have almost completely receded as has the fixed zodiac of the constellations.

It has been said that ancient man had very little space but plenty of time, whereas modern man has very little time and plenty of space since we may reach the other side of our planet in less than a day! This indeed typifies this whole trend of many millennia. Increasingly, as we have descended more deeply into the secularism of the Kali Yuga (which commenced 5 millennia ago), we have moved away from any closeness to Higher Worlds and things of the Spirit. Carl

Jung's book, *Modern Man In Search of a Soul*, describes how we now seek to reverse this dangerous one-sided orientation of awareness. We shall have to rediscover the role of the larger cosmos beyond our little planetary system, a symbolic search on the "outside" of what is also a quest "inside."

In the esoteric tradition, numbers generally have symbolic importance. Of the 10 digits, 1 and 0 are special. Of the eight digits remaining, only 2, 3, 5, and 7 are prime numbers, a prime number being divisible only by itself and 1. 2 is unique as the sole even prime. A complex number is a real number plus an imaginary number; an imaginary number is a real number times the square root of -1. In terms of complex numbers, only 3 and 7 are prime. And it is these two numbers that are so vital in the Ancient Wisdom in all of its branches.

In *The Secret Doctrine* the cosmos is presented as organized in terms of the sevenfold. A star, and thus our Sun, typifies the fourth principle of the Animal Soul, whereas the central spiritual Sun, the huge nucleus of our galaxy, is atomic and thus typifies the seventh principle. The word zoo means animal, so that the zo(o)diac pertains to the Animal Soul and the Anima Mundi. Galaxies are enormous in size with billions of stars in their population.

Therefore, this suggests that there ought to be levels of organization in the cosmos that correspond to the fifth and sixth principles. Above single stars are galactic clusters and associations, the latter looser and younger aggregations of stars than is the case with clusters. Beyond this level are the much more densely populated globular clusters in the outer halo part of a galaxy and the looser star clouds in the spiral arms of spiral galaxies such as ours is. We may assign the fifth principle of the Rational Soul or "higher mind" to the clusters and associations, and the sixth principle (Buddhi or the Spiritual Soul) to the globular clusters and star clouds. In this way the cosmos has its hierarchal organization.

I had the good fortune to study under Dr. Phyllis Ackerman of the Asia Institute. She was neither an occultist nor an astrologer and so had no axe to grind. She had discovered that in the far back preliterate period the ancients of Asia based their philosophy on cosmology. This was reflected in designs on pottery that she was the first one to explain. Most of them were water symbols based on our Milky Way Galaxy. For the ancients it was the Great Mother and source of all life, and was cosmic "water." Note that divinity was then not male but female.

Later, during the period when the Vernal Equinox was precessing slowly backward through what was later to be the constellation Gemini (about 6600 to 4400 B.C.), they spoke in Iran of the two "contending twins," which were not a mere two stars at all but rather were two large associations of stars. The benign and watery twin was the large cluster, and the O star association that surrounds it, in Orion. It is one of the most beautiful constellations in space and is very close to Earth's equator. This equates it to the "equatorial Sun" of the Kabbala which Madame Blavatsky referred to as correlated to the fifth principle, as we might anticipate.

The malign and fiery twin was the B star association in Centaurus and Lupus (far below the ecliptic and equator), and in Scorpius (constellation and not sign) near the ecliptic. This latter part they could see, that end of it being near the giant red star Antares. At its other end is the bright star Spica.

The association, termed the "Southern Stream" by astronomers, extends through about one-seventh of the circle of space and is the Via Combusta, or fiery way.

Later, in the Precessional Age of the Bull (each Age lasts about 2,150 years), as the Vernal Equinox moved back through Taurus, the Earth's North Pole pointed to Ursa Major, the Big Dipper, one of whose stars was for a time the Pole Star. The closest cluster to us is the Ursa Major Cluster of 14 stars spread out in a disk shape that cuts the galaxy via its equatorial plane into two parts. They somehow knew this, and it was in this period that the God of the Pole was accented above the Twins of the prior Age. On the plane of the ecliptic (Ursa Major is far above it), Ursa Major is some $92°$ from the Pleiades. The Pleiades are at the beginning of Taurus (constellation) and are near to the ecliptic plane. The Mahatmas give great importance to these two real clusters, as does the Tibetan, teacher of Alice Bailey and real author of her well-known book, *Esoteric Astrology*.

What Dr. Ackermann found, as did Dr. Santillana of M.I.T. and Dr. Dechend (authors of *Hamlet's Mill*) was that certain real groups of stars have been given primacy for many millennia all over the world. Near to the Pleiades are the Hyades, the second closest cluster to ours. And another important one is Praesepe (also known as the Manger or Beehive) early in the constellation Cancer. It is these key clusters and associations that are so important to us since they represent the esoteric rulerships of the zodiac as the sources of the fifth principle.

Theosophy teaches us that we are in the Fourth Chain, Fourth Round, and Fourth Globe of that Chain of Worlds so that the

Animal Soul principle predominates. But we are now in the Fifth Root Race and its Fifth Subrace, so that we are striving to move beyond the Fourth to the Fifth and its Rational Soul, typified, as the teachers said, by a Plato (a "fifth-rounder"). This is why the clusters and associations thus far mentioned, and a few others, are so vital in the "outside" world.

How then can their tremendous cosmic energies reach us?

Electric power companies build transmission lines that carry power at very high voltages such that this power must be "stepped down" via transformers in order for us to be able to apply the energy. One of the best of American astrologers, L. Edward Johndro, a radio engineer, considered that the energies of the stars filled space at light frequencies, thus enabling them to be effective over cosmic distances. As we cannot respond to such high frequencies, he believed that the planets acted as "stepdown" transformers in modulating their light-frequency "carrier wave envelopes" (i.e. Amplitude Modulation).

I am suggesting that, even more significantly, the even greater energies, both psychic and electro-dynamic, of the clusters are also transformed by the planets so that we can respond to them. Alice Bailey's teacher, hereinafter referred to as the Tibetan, indicated this also when he said that we could not respond directly, for instance. to the energies of the Pleiades.

Then, which planets are the transformers for which Cosmic Centers? Our essential thesis is that there is a chain that links us all to the Cosmos. Many students of the occult have recognized that the whirling centers of energy in the "etheric double" that both surrounds and interpenetrates our physical body correspond by position and interact with the vital endocrine glands. These energy centers are termed chakras. Johndro was the first astrologer to link the planets and their subtle spatial energies with the chakras and the endocrine glands as Mrs. Bailey did later. Thus there is a chain suggested—cosmic center to planet to chakra to endocrine gland—as the basis of "astrological influence." It was not realized that while the above is true as far as it goes, there is a crucial missing link in the chain.

My research associate, Miss Eleanor Hesseltine, and I began to realize that every planet has three epochs during the full life cycle of each individual.

The astrologer Sepharial had suggested fifty years ago that there was a preconceptual "Solar Epoch." We found that the earliest epochs are preconceptual; two-thirds of them are postnatal, which is indeed a new idea. Guided by my teacher, we found them one after the other, having had at the start of our quest no inkling that there were as many as forty-nine epochs! It was only after we had found them all that we realized that they corresponded on the time-scale of the individual to the thirty-three Subraces of Theosophy plus the sixteen more yet to come! For the pattern of the individual is not different from that of Man generically, but only the time-scale of involution and evolution differs.

We found that in addition to the Sun and Moon and the eight known planets, other than our Earth, there are seven more yet to be found, i.e. the Sun plus fifteen planets and the Moon. Dane Rudhyar in his famous *The Astrology of Personality* suggested that there might be three "higher Moons": one with a period of forty months between Mars and Jupiter in the inner part of the belt of asteroids;

one between Jupiter and Saturn; and the third one that has just been discovered between Saturn and Uranus. Chiron was discovered in the fall of 1977 in early Taurus; it has a period of about fifty years. It is a small body whose orbit links those of Saturn and Uranus.

All occult teachings recognize the reality of intramercurial Vulcan. The work of theosophists Geoffrey Hodson and George Sutcliffe in 1929 is especially important in elucidating this. Their work was published in Sutcliffe's *The New Astronomy and Cosmic Physiology*. Mr. Sutcliffe tested Mr. Hodson's powers of "etheric vision" with very successful results. Mr. Hodson then used these powers to examine our planetary system. He "saw" twelve streams of magnetic-vitalistic (pranic) energy flowing from the Sun to twelve planets. He saw all of the known planets except Pluto and Chiron, which are apparently not so linked to the Sun.

He saw Vulcan, whose radiation is only in the deep infrared part of the spectrum. So on the rare occasions when it crosses the Sun's face, as noted by the great French astronomer LeVerrier and others during the last century, we do not see Vulcan but only the absence of the visible light that it shuts off! Its period from Sutcliffe, using also the data that LeVerrier had collected, is 25.2883 days, or nearly the same as the period of the slow rotation of the Sun on its own axis.

He saw the etheric body in the asteroidal belt, this being the Rex or "king of the planets" referred to by Blavatsky and Rudhyar's Lucifer or first "higher Moon." Its radiation is ultraviolet only. He "saw" two physically densified and visible planets beyond Neptune (and Pluto), the nearer one at about 20 Scorpio, to which my teacher gave the name Morya, and the further one at about 15 Virgo as of 1929, to which she gave the name Lion. Miss Hesseltine and I confirmed the reality of all four of

these new bodies by directional tests versus events in many charts.

Is there any other confirmation of their reality? In the January 1945 issue of *Popular Astronomy*, mathematician D.E. Richardson of the Illinois Institute of Technology gave the most accurate formula to date for the distances of the planets from the Sun. It showed a "0" orbit (Vulcan) plus 12 others. The special three "higher Moons" do not appear in it, but all the known planets, including the Asteroids and Pluto, do appear, plus two beyond Pluto. These last two, which are Morya and Lion, have sidereal periods from his formula of 640 and 1610 years. This still leaves two bodies unaccounted for. We are limiting ourselves to those planets that have human epochs as there are other planets yet to be found which have no such epochs even though they are not unimportant.

William H. Pickering, a Harvard astronomer, who with Lowell successfully predicted Pluto, postulated a small body between Jupiter and Saturn (his U) which has a period of 13.93. It is the half period of this body, which I term Sigma, that accounts for the famous seven-year rhythm. I term it Sigma since it has to do with summation or endings. The last regular Postnatal Epoch before death is that of Sigma, which my teacher termed the Epoch of Accomplishment. It is more closely connected with karma than any other planet and is the "Esoteric Saturn" briefly referred to by the Tibetan.

In March 1906, Sutcliffe, writing in Alan Leo's *Modern Astrology*, had postulated four outer planets from Hindu sources. We have confirmed the reality of the two inner ones, Isis and Osiris. While Osiris has no human epoch, Isis does. Its sidereal period is probably about 384 years—based on the study by Bendandie of Magnetic storms, but currently in the Tropical zodiac is about 360 years. The late great British astrologer, Charles Carter, used this body for some fifty years. It is now in early Gemini.

For the sake of argument, let us assume that these six extra planets may be as we describe them. Why must we have not twelve but the Sun and sixteen (where the Moon can stand for the Earth itself)? On page 85 of Bailey's *Esoteric Astrology*, the Tibetan refers to the key nature of sixteen. And for that matter there is a basic rhythm in humans that has sixteen beats in twenty-four hours! There is an initial primal epoch of Chiron (like a Seed Manu at the start of a new great cycle) which is then followed by sixteen epochs in the prenatal group (birth being the seventeenth). There are sixteen regular postnatal epochs plus sixteen special postnatal epochs.

Each one of the Sun, Moon, and fourteen planets thus manifests through three epochs: one prenatal and two postnatal. Only Chiron has only one epoch. The special epochs refer to the future, meaning that response to them is limited except for those who are highly developed. Then the final regular Postnatal Epoch is the sixteenth or the thirty-third when the prenatal group is added. These figures have great relevance to the tenets of Theosophy.

10

Earlier we said that 3 and 7 were key numbers. 49 is 7 x 7. One-third of 49 is 16⅓ and two-thirds of 49 is 32⅔, which to the following whole number become 17 and 33. Mankind was "born" in the Third Subrace of the Third Root Race or in the 17th Subrace. Thus the Birth Epoch of the individual, the 17th epoch, "reflects" the pattern of generic and cosmic Man. If the seventeenth epoch refers to the crisis of birth, then the thirty-third refers to the crisis of death.

Since we are now on the Fifth Subrace of the Fifth Root Race, we are now in the 33rd Subrace! And like the individual at the Epoch of Sigma, our race is confronted with the possibility of the destruction of our planet. For the current crisis is more severe than was the case in the last days of Atlantis. My authority for this comes from the letters of Helena Roerich through whom the Agni Yoga teachings of the Lord Morya came.

In biology it is stated that "ontogenesis repeats phylogenesis," or the individual's development is a very condensed recapitulation of the much longer development of the group or phylum. During the gestation period from conception to birth, we very rapidly repeat all prior phases of biological evolution. Very briefly, we are fishlike, whereas the fish appeared half a billion years ago!

In like manner we assert that these epoch charts show our recapitulation of all previous racial psychological involution-evolution. Not only do the epochs correlate in time to the pattern of cosmic and racial involution and evolution but also in space. Let us list the orbits of our planetary system from the outermost (Lion) inward.

Lion	(Chiron)
Morya**	Sigma
Isis	Jupiter
Pluto	Rex
Neptune	Mars*
Uranus**	Venus
Chiron*	Mercury
Saturn	Vulcan

We have separated the outer planets from the inner ones. Timewise, the inner ones occur first in the prenatal group, but Mars (secular sixth ray planet) takes the place of Chiron, the never-mentioned sacred sixth ray planet. And Morya and Uranus exchange places, these being the only two anomalies. We shall see in a moment why the latter exchange occurs.

All the epochs from the first one of Chiron to the Moon's occur only on phases of the Moon and so are group epochs. A lunar epoch occurs at moonrise or moonset, or with the Moon at the upper or lower Meridian, with the exception of the C Epoch of Conception and the B Epoch of Birth, where the Moon may be anywhere. Except for the epochs of Isis and Pluto, the other eight are individual in that the Sun and Moon may be in any angular relationship. A Solar Epoch occurs at sunrise or sunset, or at noon or midnight.

The Suns of the later 10 epochs from that of the Sun to the Saturn one of birth ideally correspond in position to those Cosmic Centers for which their key planets are the "step-down transformers." The famous Enneagram is a nine-sided figure and a major mandala, one important to the

Gurdjieff Group, for instance. It actually is a combination of an equilateral triangle and a seven-sided heptagon in which there are nine instead of ten points since one corner of the triangle and one vertex of the heptagon are the same. This pivotal common point is Kether, the Crown (of the Nine Sephira of the Kabbala) and the Central Spiritual Sun or Galactic Center.

Our small planetary system is a part of three supersystems, each one inclusive on a broader scale of the one before. We and our galaxy are part of a local group of about twenty-five galaxies. It is dominated by our own large Milky Way Galaxy and by the slightly larger Andromeda Nebula, a huge spiral galaxy like our own. The centroid of mass of this local group is almost on a line with the Andromeda Nebula above the ecliptic and near the beginning of the constellation Aries of the sidereal zodiac.

At the next level down, our own galaxy's center is near the start of the constellation Sagittarius. And at the next level down is the barycenter of our local system of stars at the middle of the constellation Leo so that the three approximate an equilateral triangle. The Sun of the Lion Epoch eleven months before the B of Birth aligns with the local system (Lion was exactly there in 1929 when Hodson "saw" it!). The Sun of the Morya Epoch aligns with the local group center, and the Isis Sun aligns with the Galactic Center. Thus for those born at the beginning of August these alignments occur by conjunction, but alignments by opposition, trine, square, etc. are also significant.

In this way the three outermost planets that have human epochs bring through to us the vast energies of the three great supersystems that contain us. We are in an outer spiral arm of our galaxy, which spins for us once every 200,000,000 years as we whirl around two-thirds of the way to the edge. The local system of some 200,000 stars (the Galaxy contains 100,000,000,000 stars!) is an ellipsoidal egg-shaped entity, the real Ark that carries us over the waters (galaxy) of space, its centroid being in the antique constellation of Argo Navis—the navi-shaped Ark mentioned in a footnote in *The Secret Doctrine*.

Most of the stars we are able to see belong to this local system. Indeed, two of its major components are the Twins, the Southern Stream which centers in the Scales (the traditional center of the zodiac) and the Orion Association. The Antares end of the Fiery Twin is in the direction of the center of the Galaxy and Orion is in the direction of the anticenter, as the ancients noted. The ancients had far greater knowledge than we credit them with!

The heptagon approximately picks out other major clusters and associations—in some cases on the plane of the Ecliptic and in others on the plane of the Galactic Equator. The spacing of some epochs seven weeks apart (or one-seventh of the year) is especially applicable to seven-month children. The spacing of the Suns of the epochs for the more usual nine-month gestations is slightly different.

The Sun of the C Epoch of Conception (often termed the Lunar Epoch when only one was known) aligns with the Southern Stream Center of Uranus. About seven weeks later is the Midnight Solar Epoch of Isis (Galactic Center), and then about a month later (six and a half months before the B) is the Lunar Quarter Moon Epoch of Pluto. About four months after the C Epoch is the Animation or A Epoch of Neptune, a solar midnight one like the I Epoch; the A Chart marks the time the Soul commences to enter or "animate" the vehicle, physically the beginning of the foetal heart beat and the "quickening." Its Center is in Cygnus.

About three months before birth is the other Quarter Moon Epoch of Morya, which occurs at moonrise or moonset on an applying Moon square the Sun. Then at sunrise and very nearly seven months after the C Epoch is the Solar E Epoch of the ego and of Mars (Pleiades), when the "lucid arc" ends, according to my teacher. For it is then that the higher and lower consciousness finally separate; the prodigal son goes forth from his father's house after having drunk the waters of Lethe and "forgotten" his divine origin. Finally, under Saturn occurs the trauma of birth, which is a lunar epoch (Praesepe Cluster).

The first individual Solar Epoch is that of Lion (local system) at sunrise about eleven months before the birth chart. In the totality of the forty-eight epochs (plus the primal one) there are twelve group solar, twelve group lunar, twelve individual solar, and twelve individual epochs, so that twelve is as important a number as sixteen.

I believe that the Uranian Conception Epoch and its Southern Stream Cosmic Center correspond to the Thinking function of Jung, that the Neptunian Animation Epoch corresponds to the Feeling function of Jung (placed by us opposition Sensation and not Thinking), the center being in Cygnus which is in the constellation Capricornus when projected onto the ecliptic from far above it. The Instinctive-Intuitive function is that of the Martian E Epoch which aligns with the Pleiades, and the Saturnine Sensation function is that of birth and the Praesepe Cluster early in the constellation Cancer.

These assignments of cosmic centers are also an explanation of the Tibetan's esoteric rulerships which I find to belong to the sidereal zodiac of the constellations and not to the tropical and exoteric one of the signs. As is so often the case with such teachings, he introduced "blinds," for he correlated Saturn with Capricornus and Neptune with Cancer, or just the opposite to what we have done. In *The Secret Doctrine* we are told that Capricornus had to do with one, Solar Fire, and with two, the God of Ocean, which certainly pertains to Neptune and not to Saturn! In addition, birth is traditionally linked with the constellations of Gemini-Cancer and death with opposing Sagittarius-Capricorn.

Pluto may refer to the early part of the constellation Sagittarius and the Solar Apex or the arrow direction of our endless flight through space. While the Tibetan places Pluto in Pisces and the Moon in Virgo since he seems to have carefully reversed all even constellations, this puts the lunar center in Pisces, in agreement with our work.

But what of Pluto? From the work of Evangeline Adams, Colonel Raoul Hankar, and others, the Sun is strongest in Taurus, thus heliocentrically placing Mother Earth in the opposing sign Scorpio. Geocentrically as the Earth is at the center, it is replaced in Scorpio by Pluto. At the esoteric level the Tibetan puts the Earth in Sagittarius, which is just where our work shows that Pluto must go! On page 509 of *Esoteric Astrology* he suddenly links Pluto with the Arrow of Death, and thus with Sagittarius. Indeed, Mother Pluto is the octave of the Earth which is why our planet has been experiencing a crisis of survival in the dreaded Armageddon since the discovery of Pluto in 1930.

If one uses an Ayanamsa of 30° between the Western tropical or moving zodiac and the Eastern sidereal or fixed zodiac as of the year 2000 A.D., as I do, then the cosmic centers and their planets are as follows (given in the tropical zodiac for 2000 A.D.):

Somewhere in Aries	Unknown Center	Moon
Somewhere in Taurus	Unknown Center	Chiron
0° Gemini	Pleiades	Mars
8° Cancer	Rosette Nebula	Venus
7° Leo	Praesepe	Saturn
(14° Leo) and 15° Virgo	Local System	Lion
2° Virgo and (6° Libra)	Ursa Major	Sun
(19° Scorpio) and 26° Scorpio	Southern Stream	Uranus
26° Sagittarius	Galactic Center	Isis
3° Capricorn*	Solar Apex	Pluto
24° Aquarius*	Cygnus	Neptune
27° Aries	Local Group	Morya

The positions of Mercury and Jupiter, and Vulcan and Rex, and the Sigma Centers are as yet unknown. The ones marked with an asterisk are tentative. Those in parentheses are positions on the ecliptic that correspond to right ascension positions on the Equator, given only for bodies far from the ecliptic that have the two positions relatively far apart.

If the Sun or the key planet of a chart are conjunction or opposition in the zodiac (or "in mundo") to the related cosmic center of that epoch, that person's Soul is extra responsive to that form of cosmic energy. This provides a partial basis for a genuine arcane astrology of the Soul, which refers to the intent of the Soul for that incarnation.

In the year before birth until and including birth there are some eight epochs, of which four are solar and pertain to the indwelling entity, and four are lunar and pertain to the vehicle that is being formed for the use of that entity. The entity or egocentric being that we are normally conscious of is formed from the immortal higher self from the U Epoch of Understanding (and of Lion) eleven months before Birth until the end of the lucid arc at the E Epoch of the Ego (and of Mars) nine months later when the lower consciousness completes the separation from the higher one.

At the A Epoch of Animation, three months before the E, the entity begins to enter the vehicle—this Epoch being of Neptune. The Sun of the U Epoch opposes that of the A, and the E Epoch's Sun is at right angles to the two, thus forming a T-cross.

The fourth of these four solar epochs (the I of Isis) has its Sun only roughly opposite the E Sun so that we have an imperfect grand cross (solar). From the Lunar C Epoch (of Uranus) the Epoch of Saturn, the vehicle is formed in and by the mother and separated from her, this also taking nine months.

The Sun of the F Epoch of Fate of Morya is opposition the C Sun, and they are both square to the B Sun so that we have here a second and lunar T-cross. A high Soul may be incarnated at the F Epoch, but that is very rare, my teacher said. The Sun of the T Epoch of Ties (Pluto) is only roughly opposition the B Sun so that here too we have a very similar and imperfect grand cross (lunar).

These eight sound much like the four principles and the four faculties explored in that extraordinary book by William Butler Yeats, *A Vision*. Only that book and Bailey's rate as genuine books on esoteric astrology. It may be recalled that Yeats knew Madame Blavatsky.

Of equal if not greater interest are the sixteen regular postnatal epochs. The sequence of the prenatal ones is invariant while the sequence of the regular postnatal ones is typical and orbital out to Uranus with one anomaly. That is to say that the typical sequence is: Vulcan (during the first seven years)-Mercury-*Venus**-Moon*-Mars-*Rex*-Jupiter*-(skip Sigma)-Saturn*-*Sun*-Uranus*. Those with asterisks are solar, and those in italics are group epochs.

Since of the prenatal group (omitting Chiron's Epoch), nine are solar and seven are lunar, in this postnatal set of sixteen, nine are lunar and seven are solar. A prenatal solar epoch produces a regular postnatal lunar epoch and vice-versa.

It all has to do with the "balancing of one's Wheel"—the Wheel of Buddha's Law. In the *Mahatma Letters to A.P. Sinnett*, it was stated that the planets beyond Uranus are "extra-solar" and we find that beyond the Postnatal Epoch of Uranus, which typically occurs at about age fifty, the Epochs of the smaller bodies, Pluto*, and *Isis* occur before age thirty-five, whereas the epochs of the larger planets, Morya*, and *Lion* occur after that age. Neptune, not a small planet, has its Epoch of "Surging" usually close in time to that of Saturn. The Epoch of *Sigma* is the last one.

That of the Sun, the Epoch of Culmination, shows where the Sun of the next life will be. For most of us it is one sign earlier than the B Sun, so that, as the Tibetan says, we are on the mutable cross with the B Suns of successive lives ever earlier in the zodiac. However, for those on or nearing the Path and who seek to reverse the direction of the Great Wheel, these Suns for many lives are in the same part of space so that they are on the fixed cross. That reversal of the Wheel occurs at or near to the center of the zodiac and thus in the constellation of the Scales, being under the control of Uranus and its cosmic center in that constellation. It is no surprise that a "reversal" would be under Uranus!

The Tibetan speaks of this as "the lesser burning ground" so we see the true role of the ancient "Fiery Twin" and the later Via Combusta. Indeed, he states that First Ray Vulcan, First Ray Pluto, and Uranus are the main planets for those who have "entered the Stream" (First Initiation). At the exoteric level, Pluto is a ruler of the sign Scorpio, which corresponds to the Scales of the sidereal zodiac. Here the Disciple undergoes the fires of purification and the "death" of desire.

Postnatal epochs (I shall not try to discuss the special ones) may occur "out-of-sequence," in which case they have extra importance. In a few cases men have had Saturn Epochs, which most typically occur age 40, in their late teens. At that time they had to assume the burdens for their parents characteristics of the middle-aged! The epochs of Saturn-Uranus-Neptune, the three synthesizing planets of the Tibetan, usually take place in the 40's, when according to Carl Jung, we undergo a second major life-crisis. From the first one in the teens we tend to develop such that one of the four basic psychic functions is dominant. As a result this superior function robs the opposing inferior one of much of its psychic energy.

In the 40's the life-force seeks to make us develop the least developed part of us so that we can balance our wheel. If we meet this challenge, and many do not, then we continue to grow until we die. We have reason to believe that the postnatal epochs of these three planets time and describe this life-crisis. Indeed, the average human being long had a life expectancy of only 30 years, or one cycle of Saturn. We may surmise that Mankind is therefore now confronting this life-crisis collectively.

The capstone of our research was the discovery that one can live out more than one set of charts! My teacher stated that there were one, four, or seven, but only those in their last life on Earth—the "No Returner" of the Buddhists—experience all seven. We surmise that those on or nearing the Path experience four and that this is now more common than it was. Indeed, in this way the Soul accelerates the working off of karma.

I surmise that there are seven "lives" from one incarnation to the next one. If only one "life" is lived in one physical incarnation, then six must be lived through between incarnations such that the interval between lives is longer. From the Agni Yoga Teachings of the Lord Morya, the average interval of both incarnate (40 years) and discarnate (660 years) existence is 700 years. Earlier in time it was longer. Those with four lives in one, the true Brahmins or "twice-born," experience only three "lives" discarnately. As one "life" is forty-nine epochs, then seven of them equals 343 (seven cubed). If to this we add the seventeen in the prenatal set we have 360 or the number of degrees in the zodiac, a curious thing.

Such in brief is the outline of a possible basis for a real arcane astrology. It is by no means wholly theoretical. All of these charts can be tested by the experienced and possibly skeptical competent professional astrologer. They—some of them—have been used by me for twenty-nine years in actual practice.

Any postnatal epoch times the onset of a new chapter in one's life. If several occur close together in time, then one's life undergoes a major change. The special postnatal epochs are especially significant for new forms of creativity or for some vital change in the focus of consciousness; they are less tied to the event level.

If sixteen factors plus the Sun comprise any valid human epoch chart, then we may surmise that a set of forty-nine charts (based on sixteen factors plus a special one) comprise a higher entity, the Mandala of the Soul, perhaps. I have found that there is a limit to what one can tell about any individual from any one chart. They are actually different facets of one jewel which is that Soul Mandala.

It is the relationships among the charts in the super-chart that alone can tell us about the higher or Soul part of the individual. It took me a long time to reach this simple but very vital realization. It is the relationship of the Postnatal Sun of the Epoch of the Sun to the Prenatal B Sun that tells us in which direction that individual's Wheel is revolving, to give only one example. I believe that it will be in this direction that we must pick our way to make a reverent approach to the astrology of the Soul.

Chapter Two

The Astrology
of the Soul

My main purpose here is to give some examples so as to enable the reader to determine seven of the prenatal charts plus one regular postnatal chart, the Mars Chart of Purpose. Most of us do not yet respond fully to the Isis Chart.

The basic premise is that there are stages in the Descent of the Soul to the body and that charts can be made for each stage. They are alternately solar and lunar in nature; vowel symbols are used for solar epochs and consonants for lunar epochs.

The lunar epochs have mainly to do with the vehicle (body). The first individual lunar chart ("individual" meaning that the Sun and Moon may be in any relationship) is that of conception ©), also known as the Lunar Epoch, which is the sole lunar epoch known to astrologers until now. The C Epoch averages about nine months before the Birth (B) Chart, which is also a lunar epoch.

At the C Epoch in one's higher consciousness (Soul), one assumes responsibility for the development of one's vehicle. Uranus is the key body of the C Epoch Chart, which shows how one thinks and "conceives" things. The next lunar epoch, the T Epoch of Ties, occurs about six and a half months before the B Chart on an applying quarter Moon and with the Moon usually in an upper culmination (occasionally the Moon is at the IC).

Abortions or miscarriages occur at or near the T Epoch; Pluto is the key planet of this epoch, and we see it here as the eliminator. The next lunar epoch, the F Epoch of Fate, occurs also on an applying quarter Moon at moonrise or moonset about three months before the birth. The F Epoch is the first at which one can be born (very rarely). Its key planet, Morya, has yet to be discovered. William H. Pickering, one of the two astronomers who predicted where Pluto would be found, gave the correct position for it in early Scorpio at the beginning of the 20th century. The F Epoch shows what one has to "transmute" (the "blows of fate" or karma) in life. The T and F charts may be done even if the birth time is unknown. At the B Epoch the vehicle is separated from the mother, and we enter the limited domain of the dense physical world, the key planet being Saturn.

The Solar Epochs U, I, A, and E refer to the indwelling entity, and thus to the life force (Soul) which uses the body. Just as the mother grows a small body inside herself, so the Soul forms a small part of its psychic energy so as to create the egocentric lower consciousness. This process commences at the U Epoch of Understanding, eleven months before the B Chart, and is completed at the E Epoch of the ego two months before the birth. Just as it averages nine months (B Sun square C Sun on an average) from the C to the B Epoch, so it averages nine months from the Solar U Epoch to the Solar E Epoch.

The key planet of the U Epoch is the furthest one from the sun that is linked to it by a stream of magnetic-vitalistic energy, according to the Theosophist seer, Geoffrey Hodson. This planet, Lion, in Virgo, is the planet of education and civilization, the collective attempt to raise consciousness through interaction with form. Although both the U and C Epochs are "mental", the C Epoch of the Thinking function differs from the U (of synthesis and integration) in that, like its key planet Uranus, it gives the power of original thought.

The I Epoch of Isis (the next major planet beyond Pluto, which was used by the late Charles Carter for fifty years) occurs about seven and a half months before the birth chart. It is through the I Epoch that we seek reunion with our higher consciousness. At the A Epoch of Animation (the "quickening" and start of the foetal heartbeat) the Soul commences to enter the vehicle, as the Buddhists teach. This is about five months before the B. The key planet of the A Epoch is Neptune, its chart being the main one of feeling and emotion. Though both the I and the A Epochs relate to feeling and emotion, the I Epoch is fiery and of the heart, while A is watery and tends towards sentimentality.

The A and I Epochs, both being solar, occur near midnight. The E Epoch of ego is keyed to Mars and expresses instinct and, at a higher level, intuition. At the E Epoch, the U and E Epochs being the sole individual sunrise ones in the prenatal set, the final separation of the lower from the higher consciousness occurs—the drinking of the waters of Lethe

27

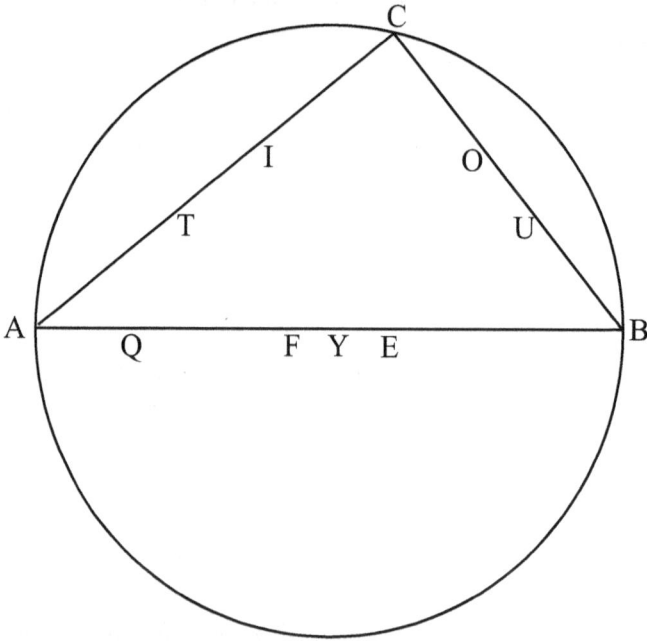

Figure 1

which causes us to "forget" our Father in Heaven and to go forth as the prodigal Son from His home. The E and B Charts are more mundane and extrovertive than the I and A Charts.

Figure 1 is a diagram that illustrates the spacing of the Suns of these epochs for normal births (prematures have a slightly different pattern that corresponds to a seven-sided heptagon).

We draw a circle with a horizontal diameter of 5 units, the left hand end being A and the other end B. From A we then draw a line to the circumference above the diameter at C that is 4 units long, for the angle at C is a right angle. We are using the perimeter of this ABC right triangle instead of the circumference of a circle. The 3 + 4 + 5 = 12 units is the length of the perimeter. The 12 stands for twelve months, signs, or constellations.

The letter C stands for the C Sun and four months later (average) is the A Sun at A. Five months or signs after this along the longest (hypotenuse) side of the triangle is birth at B (B Sun). The key planets of these three epochs are Neptune, Saturn, and Uranus, which are described in Alice Bailey's *Esoteric Astrology* as the three synthesizing planets. But they also correspond to three of the four basic psychic functions of Carl Jung: A, Emotion, Feeling; B, Sensation; and C, Thinking. How then do we find the fourth one?

We bisect the right angle at C and extend the bisecting line to an intersection with the side AB at E. This then becomes the position of the E Sun of Intuition and Instinct, the fourth basic psychic function. It is $4.3°$ short of just seven signs or months after the C Sun, this interval being less variable than the others. All the values we give are average or Saturnine ones. One must also allow for the second moment of a statistical distribution which is termed the variance (Uranus) about the Mean (first moment).

If the angle at B is bisected, the bisecting line reaches the side CA at I, just $45°$ after the C Sun, which is where the I Sun is located on an average. The side BC is different from the other two since in time it cannot bring us back from the B to C Epoch. Thus the bisection of the angle at A gives the O Sun at $0°$, which, while $40°$ before the C Sun, is in time one year plus

40° before the C Epoch. The center of our original circle at Y marks the place of the Y Epoch, or the first one of all, 13 years and 2.5 months before the B. (All lunar phase, or group epochs, have their letters underlined.)

Now, as the E Sun is 10.7° from the Y Sun, might there not be another one 10.7° on the other side of that Y Sun? There is and this is the F Sun just 4.3° from the opposition to the C Sun, so that the C opposition F square B Suns make a lunar T-Cross! In like manner the U Sun is 4.3° from the opposition to the A Sun and via their square to the E Sun they make a solar T-Cross (the U Sun is 25.7° after the B Sun).

The I Sun is 15° from the middle of the side CA so that the T Sun is 15° on the other side of the center of that side, i.e., 45° before the A Sun. Finally, the Q Epoch of the Moon (the O Epoch is that of the Sun) has its Sun 115.7° before the B Sun but is not a mere four months before the B Epoch—rather, it is one year plus four months. We shall not concern ourselves here with the O and Q Epochs, which are like the T and F, since they can be done even if the birth time is unknown. These group epochs refer to various kinds of group karma.

In the prenatal set of sixteen epochs there are only two for the quarter Moon, the T and F of Pluto and Morya. In the postnatal set of thirty-two epochs there are again only two for the quarter Moon, those of Lion and Isis. The four outermost planets are Pluto, Isis, Morya, and Lion, in that order.

Thus only the outermost planets have Quarter Moon Epochs. These four planets bring through, as stepdown transformers, the energies of the great Cosmic Triangle and Pluto refers to the Galactic Apex. We may consider them to refer to transcending functions just as Mars, Saturn, Uranus, and Neptune refer to basic functions.

We use the E Epoch of Mars to cope with the challenges of the F Epoch of Morya; the B Epoch of Saturn to deal with the problems of the U Epoch of Lion; the A Epoch of Neptune to handle the needs of the I Epoch of Pluto; and the C Epoch of Uranus to embrace the depths of the I Epoch of Isis.

Thus the fourfold becomes the eightfold, which is notable in Tibetan thinking and also in that extraordinary book by William Butler Yeats: *A Vision*. In it we find the Four Faculties and the Four Principles.

Figure 2 (page 32) shows the Suns of the eight epochs plus the Y Sun on the circumference of a circle, one's own personal zodiac. The T Sun makes with the lunar T-cross an imperfect grand cross, and the I Sun makes with the solar T-cross an imperfect grand cross. A perpendicular line through the Y Sun divides the circle into two parts: a light half—E, B, U, O, and C Suns (the B-U Epochs thus the most overt)—and a dark half—the I, T, A, Q, and F Epochs (the I and A the most covert, intangible).

If we look back at Figure 1 we find the A, E, and B Suns of the individual epochs on the long, or base, side. They are the most basic and most people respond to them. Unless people are intellectually developed, there is less response to the C Epoch and the U Epoch. My hypothesis is that those who are still more primitive than civilized "integrate" themselves via the Sunrise E Epoch and function mainly via the side AEB. Those who are genuinely civilized and educated, the Thinkers, function mainly via the side BUC and integrate them-

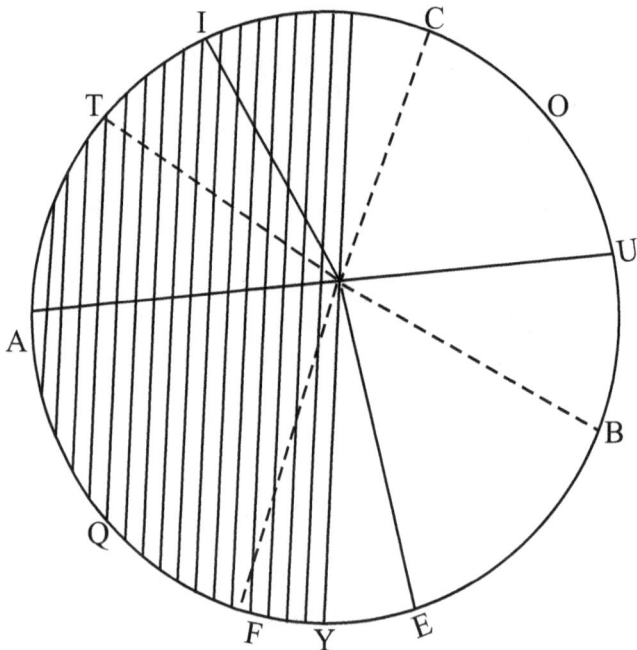

Figure 2

selves through the Sunrise U Epoch. The spiritually elite
function mainly via the side CIA and integrate themselves
via the I Epoch. My teacher stated that at a very advanced
level the E Epoch changed from sunrise to midnight, whereas
the I Epoch changed from midnight to sunrise.

All of these charts may be done without any reference to
metaphysics. It is preferable that astrologers who are competent but skeptical as to cloudy metaphysics should work with
these charts in contrast to those lovers of the esoteric, who
hardly deserve the name of astrologer! For one must be a

competent astrologer to do these charts. Knowing their Laws is only the first step as one may easily do the "wrong" chart. My wife's book, *Aspects to Horoscope Angles*, will help, as will *The Technique of Rectification* (included in *The Best of Charles Jayne*), wherein both validation and rectification methods are discussed. The tools that Miss Eleanor Hesseltine, my chief collaborator, and I used were secondary progression plus solar, Ascendant, and vertical arc directions in both longitude and declination, and both converse and direct. They are fully described in My *Progressions and Directions*. It is highly advisable that at least two competent and experienced astrologers should work together on these charts so as to minimize errors of various kinds.

Chapter Three

Procedure for Prenatal Charts

There are four major steps in the determination of any one of these prenatal charts. First, one uses the Laws of the Sun, Moon, Angles and Sex to cast the chart. Obviously if your mother says that you arrived two weeks late you don't set up your C Chart of Conception for nine months but instead for as close to nine months as you can get. These Epoch Charts do not necessarily coincide exactly with the related biological moments. The main criterion is astrological. The C Epoch may occur hours or even days from the exact date and time of the fertilization of the ovum by the sperm. The biological moment, whether of Conception, "quickening" (start of foetal heartbeat) or Animation, or of birth itself, is secondary.

If you have a choice between two dates for a C Chart—one a little early, one a little late and two weeks after the first one when the Moon is on the opposite side of the zodiac—consider the planetary pattern carefully as to which one fits best with the way in which that person typically thinks and "conceives" things. Or it may be that you are pretty sure of the date but are not certain whether to put the C Ascendant conjunction the B Moon or opposition to it. This assumes that in both cases the C Moon is within a permissible orb (maximum 6-7′30″) of a conjunction or opposition to the B Ascendant *and* that your B Ascendant is accurate! In this case you study the house positions of the planets and the aspects to the angles in order to determine which fits the best.

Fairly often you will not be sure that the chart you have done is correct. Then you apply the second test. You take arcs of direction (solar arc in both longitude and declination) and progression (secondary) of the Lights with the planets (they are stronger than the merely interplanetary ones) to see if they correlate to the appropriate life events. If there is no correlation at all (people won't remember all events), then the chart is invalid. In *The Technique of Rectification* I give an example for finding a C chart; both correct and incorrect charts are included.

It is vital to know that Moon-angle interchanges between charts need not be exact, as L. Edward Johndro found after studying 200 obstetrical cases from the Flower Hospital in New York City. The insistence by Sepharial and E. H. Bailey that such Band C interchanges must be exact did much harm to the whole study of such epochs. Margaret Hone rejected the C Chart since in very high terrestrial latitudes certain degrees cannot rise. If your B Moon is at 25° Gemini, for instance, that position or the opposite one cannot be on the C Ascendant in, say, Tromso, Norway. George Bailey (not to be confused with E.H. Bailey), writing on "Polar Prenatalistics" in *Astrology* (1955-56), showed that one can replace the Ascendant in such cases with the Equatorial Ascendant (mistakenly termed the East Point). If any prenatal chart, from the C to the E inclusive, occurs at a different place than that of birth, see later in this chapter for information on what to do.

If the gestation period was from six and a half to eight months, the B and C lunar interchanges are with the Vertex instead of the Ascendant. It is assumed that such "prematures" are "born" at their E Epochs, which, of course, are no longer sunrise charts.

Let us assume that you have found a C Chart (or other prenatal chart) that passes the first two tests. Then the third test is to rectify its angles—easier to do than with most B Charts since it can't be off more than a few degrees.

The C Ascendant averages about a half degree from the exact conjunction or opposition to the B Moon in our experience. The B Ascendant is off four degrees on an average. Johndro and his partner, the late W. Kenneth Brown, did some 200 to 250 C Charts. My chief collaborator in this research, Miss Eleanor Hesseltine, and I have done an equal number.

Doing the C Chart correctly is essential since its angles determine the positions of the Moons of the A, E, and B Charts, which is helpful in predicting birth and in determining the "true" birth chart. One does not bother to try to rectify any prenatal chart until it has passed the first two tests, for you won't be able to if it is the wrong one!

The final and fourth test is your ability to forecast with the chart you have done. It may be asked what is the difference between an aspect to, say, the Midheaven of a C Chart and a B Chart? They both are effective at the event level. An aspect of stress to your B Midheaven may correlate to the loss of a job and it can mean the same thing in aspect to the C Midheaven.

The C Midheaven differs from the B Midheaven in that it has to do with what you think about your career or status (Midheaven) whereas in the B Chart the Midheaven is more tangible. The aspect of stress to the C Midheaven not only may bring the loss of a position but also a loss or lessening in how you "conceive" your status and your career. In an A Chart it would be more a matter of how you feel or "emote" about your career, etc.

Next I shall give examples of the U, C, A, E, and F Mars Charts of a certain woman. I will not give her B Chart in order to protect her identity, but will give its Lights and angles so as to enable us to find her U and C Charts. Those are the two you can do (plus the I) if you have an accurate B Chart. The B time was given to the nearest minute and has been checked astrologically.

Once the C has been done, one may do the A and E, which are shown next. Finally we show the F and the regular Postnatal Mars Chart of Purpose. The F can be done even if the time of birth is unknown, and it helps in doing the Mars Chart. One reason for choosing her epoch charts is that they are typical, in the spacing apart of the Suns, of the standard pattern.

I shall refer to our example person as X. X was born November 3, 1941, with a Sun at 10°29′ Scorpio, a Moon at 1°55′ Taurus, an Ascendant at 14°07′ Virgo, a Midheaven at

11°04' Gemini, and a Vertex at 16°49' Aquarius. The location of birth is 41N10, 79W52.

Doing the prenatal charts in their temporal order (skipping only the I and T̲) we shall first do the U Chart of Understanding, of "sober second thought," of learning and learned responses (as contrasted with the other Sunrise or E Chart of unlearned or instinctual responses). The U Sun is more likely to be less than 25.7° later than the B Sun than it is to be more than that amount. I have yet to find a U Sun that is more than 180° from the A Sun. The Law of the Sun is that the U Epoch occurs slightly over eleven months before the B. The Law of the Moon is that the U Moon is conjunction or opposition the B Vertex. Since the B Vertex is at 16°49' Aquarius, the U Moon ought to be at or near mid-Leo or mid-Aquarius.

I first tried December 4, 1940 with the Sun at 12°14' Sagittarius and the Moon at 17°58' Aquarius. The other possibility was two weeks earlier (November 21, 1941) with the Sun at 29°03' Scorpio and the Moon at 14°17' Leo. In both cases the Sun is s lightly above the Ascendant (Law of Sex) since X is female, and it is a Sunrise Chart (Law of the Angles).

The Chart tried first had a very close conjunction of Mars-Venus at 9-10° Scorpio opposition Saturn at 9°03' Taurus and Jupiter at 6°52' Taurus from the late eleventh to the late fifth houses. I use and prefer Campanus houses. This configuration did not seem to fit this individual. Indeed, Pluto at 4°08' Leo made a T-cross with it from the eighth House. The Midheaven was at about 2° Libra. Solar arc directions of Venus and Mars to a conjunction of the Sun and of Saturn, and Jupiter opposition, did not correlate to events in her life. It was rejected.

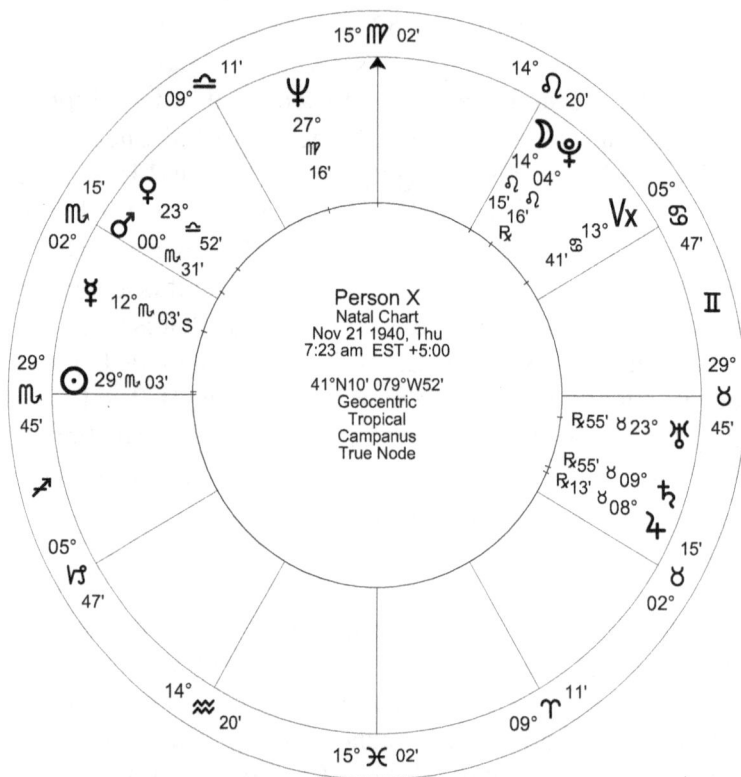

Figure 1, U Chart

It so happens that the C and A Charts had been done first, which helped. The A Sun was at 9°21′ Gemini so that the point opposite this is at 9° Sagittarius. Then the fact that the first U Sun was later in the zodiac than this point suggested that the chart might not be valid. On an average, the U Sun would be 4.3° earlier than this point, or at about 5° Sagittarius. The actual U Sun at 29° Scorpio is less than a week earlier. The first chart shown is this U Chart in Figure 1.

A long move was made in February 1969 due to the death of her father-in-law; solar arc Mars was conjunct the Sun in early January 1969, and the Sun rules part of the eighth house (death of a man) and the first part of the ninth (long move).

By a slow vertical arc direction she had Saturn opposition Sun nearly three months before the death of her maternal grandfather on October 9, 1967. Saturn came from the sixth house of health. We can employ vertical arc even before rectification since the Vertex is in the sign Cancer where, like the Ascendant, it moves slowly so that the length of its arc changes but slowly. She had solar arc Pluto square the Sun in April 1965; it would square the Ascendant later (say three to nine months, depending upon the rectification). Her mother (Pluto) had a gall bladder operation on July 21, 1965.

She has a strong ninth house interest in life, i.e., books, metaphysics, astrology, etc. and we note the Moon at the cusp of the ninth house. Indeed, there is a strong fixed T-cross of Mercury in Scorpio in the twelfth opposition Jupiter and Saturn in Taurus in the sixth, all square to the Moon and Pluto in the eighth house. Note that Mercury is now in the T-cross, whereas in the other chart it was Venus-Mars.

This fits much better with her and the nature of this Chart. I assume that the chart is valid. Some of the aspects of the rectification (stage three) were as follows:

Vertical arc Uranus was square Midheaven (comes from late in the sixth where it affects the seventh) on June 28, 1970 on the final separation from her husband. Mercury is the main ruler of that seventh house and came by Ascendant arc to the conjunction of the Ascendant at her marriage on May 7, 1964

41

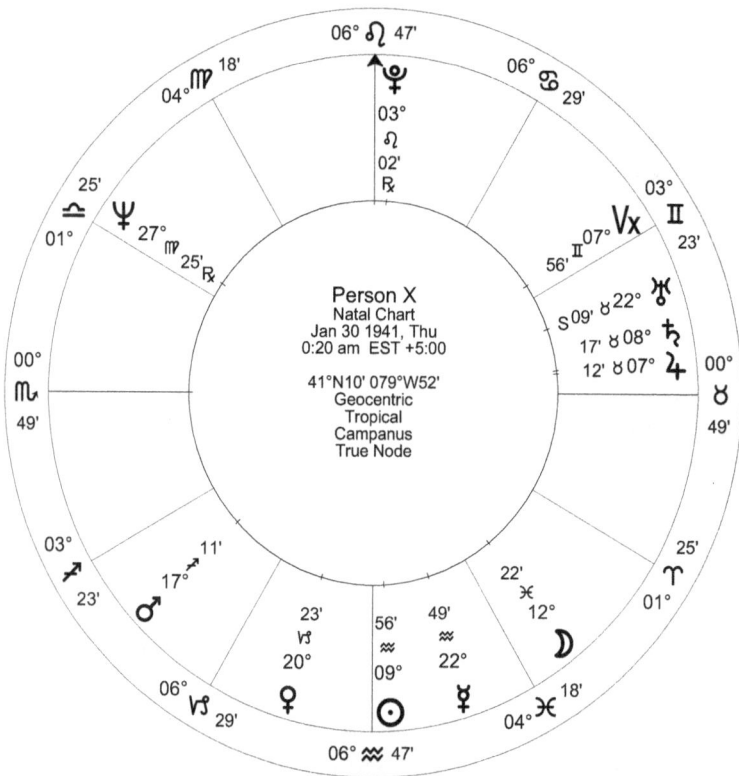

Figure 2, C Chart

(and for many months before that was moving from the conjunction to the Sun).

The "key" planet Lion is at 18°03′ Virgo in the tenth and conjunct the Midheaven radically. This is indicative of the importance to her life of not only learning but teaching, which she does in her career.

The first prenatal chart that I did was her C Chert. From the Law of the Sun, the C Sun ought to be at 10-11° Aquarius in square to her B Sun at 10°29′ Scorpio, since she was a normal nine-month baby. From the Law of the Moon, the Moon ought to be at or near 14° Pisces or Virgo. If we place the C Ascendant opposition her natal Moon, and thus at about 2° Scorpio, her C Sun is at 9°56′ Aquarius in very close square to her B Sun. So this is probably the right day.

With this Ascendant the C Moon is at 14°16′ Pisces or only 0°09′ from an opposition to her B Ascendant. If we take an early Taurus Ascendant, then the C Moon, half a day earlier or half a day later, will be about six degrees from the opposition to the B Ascendant (too wide). It is probable *a priori* that this then is the correct chart. Its date was January 31, 1941.

The Pluto-Midheaven conjunction from the end of the ninth gives not only investigative ability but also a dominant mother (Pluto). Its opposition to the fourth house Sun, among other things, indicates men who are devious (Pluto-Sun) and have ties with other women (Pluto-Sun). This opposition is square the opposition of the cuspal Scorpio Ascendant to the Jupiter-Saturn conjunction in the seventh house. Under such a fixed grand cross she would be unusually fixed as to her ideas and concepts.

On top of it all, the key planet Uranus in the seventh house is contraparallel to that Sun in its sign Aquarius, which would be difficulty in marriage due to different ideas (Uranus-Sun in C Chart). The close square to that Aquarian Mercury from Uranus (orb of 0°40′) gives the ability to think in original ways and to be somewhat of an independent thinker. It is a strong chart.

She had solar arc Jupiter trine Sun (but radical square) in early July 1974, not far from the date of a move (May 26, 1973) that involved a new and bigger (Jupiter) apartment (Sun in the fourth). She became engaged to a saturnine man on solar arc Saturn trine Sun (but radical square) in early June 1972 (which wasn't to work out) and moved in August 1972 to an older (Saturn) building, which wasn't to work out in accordance with her conceptions (or preconceptions) either.

The solar arc Sun conjunction the Moon of December 1972 brought a marked man-woman compatibility in January 1973. On Sun quincunx Pluto by solar arc (but radical opposition) in December 1963, she met her husband-to-be. He was devious (Pluto) as there was another woman (Pluto-Sun). The chart had passed the first two tests.

On C Midheaven (always moved by solar arc in longitude or in declination) trine that seventh house Saturn (but radical square) in April 1972, a woman partner who was a Capricorn (Saturn) was eliminated from a business (Midheaven) partnership (seventh house).)All the charts given have been rectified.) On Midheaven quincunx Sun (but radical opposition) at the beginning of November 1973 she had differences in ideas © Chart) with her male boss (Sun rules Midheaven) as to career (Midheaven) and was unable to get her way in the matter.

I should remark that the ninth house Pluto is an index to problems with a female (Pluto), a sister-in-law (ninth house). On Pluto sextile the Ascendant, which it rules, in late July 1968 there were psychological problems in her marriage. On Neptune conjunction the Ascendant by solar arc in June 1974

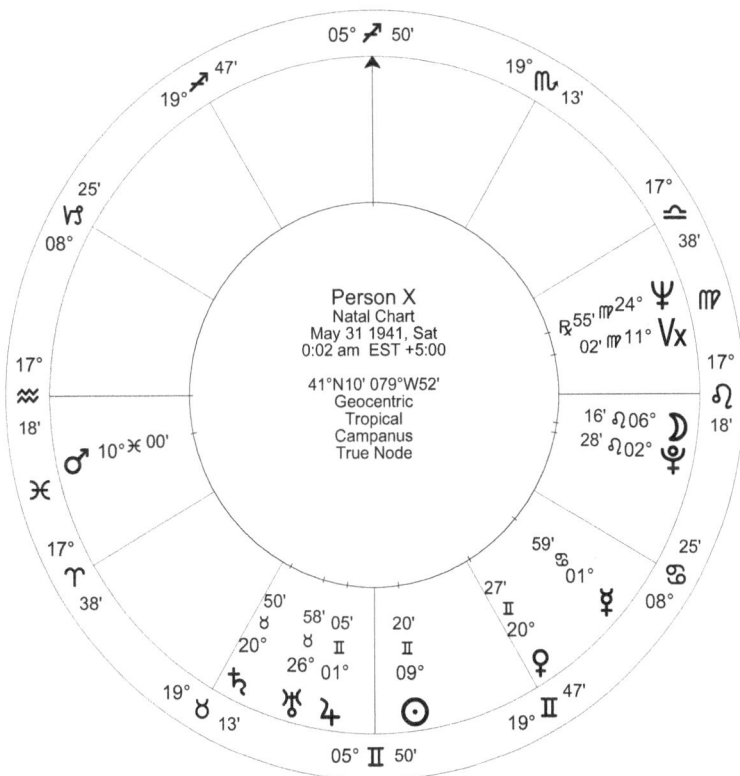

Figure 3, A Chart

(coming from the eleventh), she participated in an inspiring group event as to ideas. I assume that the chart is valid and rectified.

The Law of the Sun for the A Chart is five months before the B or four months after the C—varies from three and a half to five months after the C. If it typifies the Law of the Sun, the A Sun will be at about 10° Gemini and, from the Law of the

Moon (A Moon conjunction or opposition the C Midheaven), the A Moon will be at about 7° Leo or Aquarius. At a few minutes after midnight on May 31, 1941 the Sun was at 9°21' Gemini and the Moon at 6°08' Leo.

This then is a probable A Epoch. In doing it we debated—my wife who is an excellent astrologer helped with the C, A, and E Epochs—as to whether we should make the A Epoch two weeks later with its late Gemini Sun square the key planet, Neptune, in the seventh house. We concluded that she was probably not that mixed up about men! X admits to being a romantic, so note the fifth house Venus in Gemini square the seventh house Neptune in Virgo.

The Pluto-Moon conjunction in the sixth house with the Moon contraparallel the Ascendant fits her mother (Pluto), who has had considerable difficulties with her reproductive system (Pluto in the sixth). X has attracted masculine and aggressive men to her (as shown by the first house Mars in Pisces closely square the Sun). Such a man entered her life on solar arc Mars sextile Sun (but radical square) in March 1972 and went out of it, after a fight (Mars), at the beginning of July 1973, on Sun trine Mars (by solar arc) which again set off that trying radical square.

He also helped her to move then (fourth House Sun). This contributed much to the second stage validation of the chart. The recent transits of Neptune over the A Midheaven and then opposition its Sun in 1973-75 brought some emotional quandaries, and about men and marriage as one might anticipate, since this is the key planet which has extra weight in its chart—just as Grant Lewi found Saturn to have in the B Chart via its transits.

46

Her paternal grandfather died October 17, 1969, one month after Saturn was trine the Ascendant at 17°50′ Aquarius, and set off the radical square by solar arc. She had first moved away from home in October 1962 due to work, with Ascendant opposition Neptune by Ascendant arc the following month. Events can lead a Neptune direction but always lag a Saturn one.

The significant thing was not so much the move as the emotional wrench (Neptune) of leaving home. She rather quickly moved back to her home town on Uranus trine Ascendant, but radical square by solar arc, at the beginning of April 1963. The chart was set as to its angles on this since Uranus is the most accurate planet. We assume then that this chart is valid and rectified.

The next epoch is the Epoch of Fate. An F Chart is described in the section of *The Technique of Rectification* (included in *The Best of Charles Jayne*), that is devoted to dealing with unknown birth times. You are referred to the discussion there. In the winter 1971-72 issued of *The Astrological Review* of the Astrologers' Guild of America, Inc., an article of mine was published on this chart, referring to a woman who came to me with a completely unknown birth time. I have rectified unknown times of birth but it is very difficult.

One can do an F Chart in such cases as I have done from time to time since Miss Hesseltine and I discovered it on November 1, 1952. The Law of the Sun is that the epoch occurs three months less 4.3°, or about eighty-seven days before the B. Its Sun is usually fairly closely opposition the C Sun, more often a little over 180° after it than a little less than 180°.

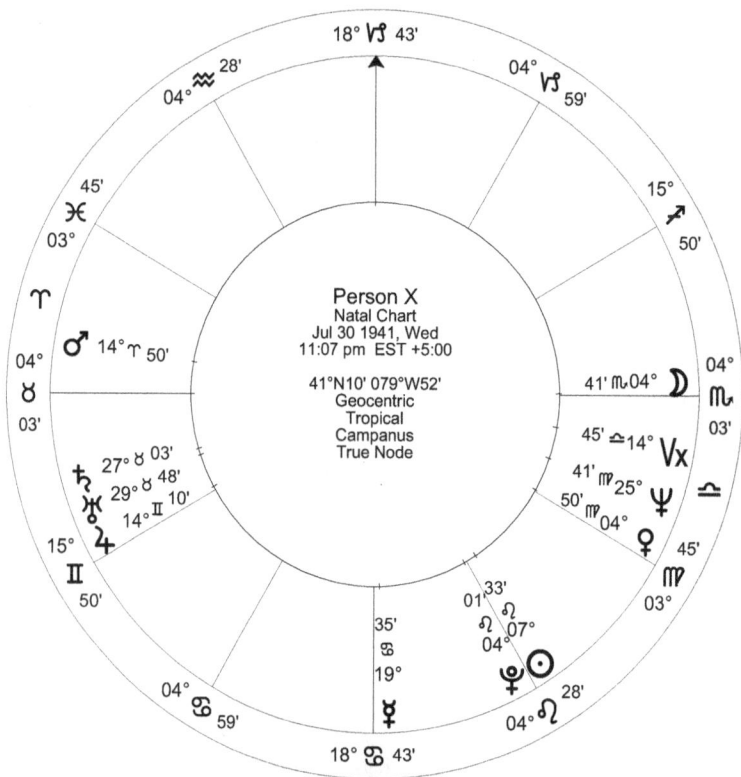

Figure 4, F Chart

The Law of the Moon is that it must occur on a quarter Moon with the Moon applying as closely as possible to the square of the Sun; it must not separate.

The Law of the Angles is that it must occur at moonrise or moonset. The Law of Sex is that it usually has the Moon about half a degree below the Ascendant or above the Descendant for a woman (and thus angular), or half a degree above the Ascendant or below the Descendant for a man (and thus cadent), before the chart is rectified.

Miss L., whose F Chart I am writing about, had traveled more than any client I have known in over a quarter of century of practice. Therefore, even though this chart is a group one, which others share with one, it would have to show that kind of emphasis in its pattern. The unknown planet Hermes has as much to do with travel as do the Moon and Uranus, but as the Moon must rise or set we can't find it in the ninth house.

Born June 9, 1915, her F Chart took place March 23, 1915 at 112W30, 45N50 (geocentric) and has Uranus at 14°19′ Aquarius, the Campanus cusp of the ninth being 14° Aquarius. Sesquiquadrate Uranus is 29°19′ Gemini. The Ascendant was rectified to 28°09′ Gemini and the Moon was at 29°38′ (their Midpoint falls at 28°53′ Gemini). The Sun is at 2°00.8′ Aries and this is square the Sun and Ascendant. Forty-five degrees from that Sun brings us to 17°01′ Aquarius with Hermes (or "K") at 17°18′ Aquarius. The Venus at 19°38′ Aquarius shows the love of travel. The Midheaven was at 29°33′ Aquarius. With Saturn at 25°59′ Gemini ruling virtually all of the seventh house and an integral part of the square of the Sun to the Ascendant conjunction Moon conjunction Pluto (at 0°10′ Cancer), it is not surprising that she was still single at age fifty-six. The chart is certainly valid!

In the F Chart of X, the B Sun less 85.7° gives about 15° Leo. Therefore, it could be one week later or one week earlier. I tried the later one at 21°31′ Leo, but it proved to be wrong. Although, with the Sun-Mercury-Pluto in the ninth, it might have been valid.

The Moon was setting at 17°57' Taurus and Saturn was conjunction Uranus at the end of Taurus in square to the Midheaven at about 28° Leo. This could have been right too due to the marital difficulties. But its aspects by direction to and by the Lights did not correspond to major events. So the F Chart two weeks earlier was tried with the Moon at 4°41' Scorpio and again at moonset, but now with the Sun at 7°33.3' Leo early in the fifth House. This one appeared to be correct. Its Mercury at 19°36' Cancer opposite the Midheaven fits with her career activities, which have been predominantly Mercurial. And the Pluto-Sun conjunction square the Moon fits with the types of experiences that she has had to transmute (nature of F Chart).

She moved in late May 1973 with Pluto sextile the Moon (ruling the fourth), but radically square, in late June 1973. She had the Moon (from the seventh) trine Pluto (radically square), with Pluto ruling the seventh, in early February 1972 and broke off with a woman partner in April 1972. The above aspects were both by solar arc. About a month after her marriage she had, by the faster Ascendant arc, Pluto sextile the Moon (radically square) as indicative of her husband's tie (Pluto) with another woman. Some months before this, Pluto, by the same arc, was trine the Ascendant (radical square), with Pluto ruling the seventh—all of this referring to her marriage (seventh house) and the problems connected to it. It appeared to have passed the first two tests and was then rectified.

Secondary Mercury trine Midheaven, but radical opposition, in late September 1972, brought the end of a job in November 1972. The Midheaven progressed by solar declination arc to a square of Saturn in early October 1972 also showed this.

The new job of October 8, 1974 is close to the Midheaven square Uranus by solar declination arc.

At the end of March 1969 on Sun trine Ascendant, but radically square, she moved back to her home town. She had just previously moved away on the death of her father-in-law so that the state of the man in her life (Sun), her husband, was the main consideration.

In November 1972, solar arc Pluto was trine the Ascendant, radical square, being the ruler of the Scorpionic seventh house. In the following month, on the 25th, she broke the engagement.

I strongly suggest that this F Chart be tried as it can be quite useful. Like the other Quarter Moon Epoch (the T Chart), it will not show deaths. The much more psychological T Epoch occurs about six and a half months before the B, with the Moon usually conjunction the Midheaven, and occasionally opposite it. Two of the cases of such lower culmination Moons occurred for a primal therapist and a medium, i.e., for those who are closer than most to the unconscious depths and the realm of the psyche. The T Chart is the chart of psychological ties.

The E Chart is next in the stages in the descent of the Soul to this saturnine realm of time and space. By the Law of the Sun, the E Sun is 64.3° before the B Sun, but more reliably 205.7° after the C Sun. Using this last would put it for X at about 5°30′ Virgo. A sunrise chart (the Law of the Angles gives a sunrise solar chart) on August 29, 1941 puts the Sun at 5°41.6′ Virgo and the Moon at 3°53′ Sagittarius in the fourth house.

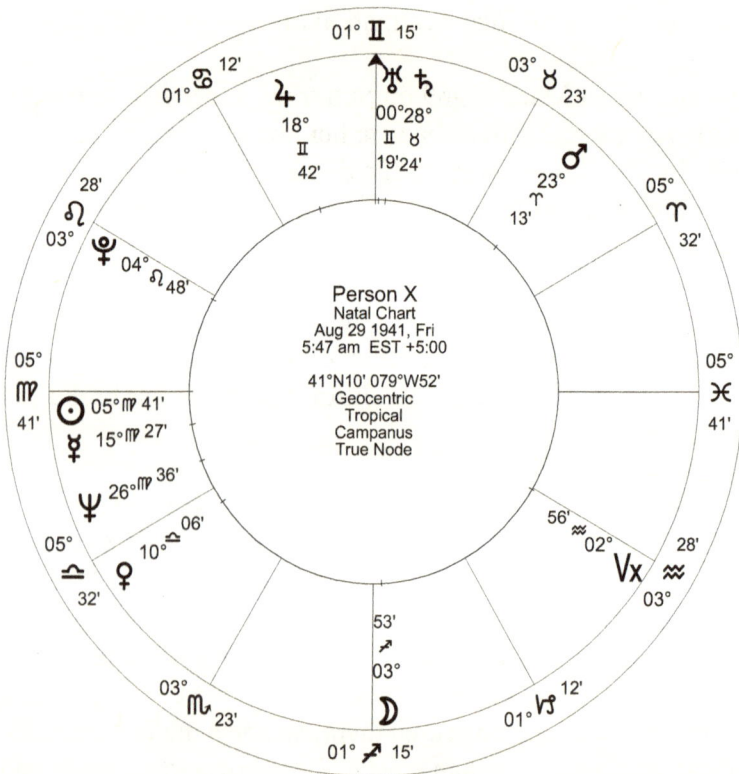

Figure 5, E Chart

From the Law of the Moon (E Moon conjunction or opposition the C Vertex of 7°58′ Gemini) the E Moon is about four degrees from an opposition to her C Vertex so that the Chart is probably valid on purely technical grounds.

Uranus and Saturn at the end of the ninth are conjunction the Midheaven, opposition the Moon, and square the Sun and Ascendant. This is a potent mutable T-cross, which gives her a drive for independence (Uranus) that is somewhat muffled by the Saturn. The key planet, Mars, is at 23°14' Aries in the eighth house, which it rules, and is antiscion the Sun and Ascendant—a kind of parallel.

It is notable that of the Midheavens of her individual charts (omitting the T and F), four are in mutable signs, one is in a fixed sign (C), and none are in a cardinal sign. Her job record is one of many changes, therefore. Since this is the chart of basic animal drive as well as of instinctive sense of direction (and intuition) and of unlearned responses, she has a strong persistence in spite of the apparent mutability.

The solar arc Sun conjunction Neptune of March 1963 was followed by her return home at the end of March. At the end of June 1970 she moved and separated from her husband, with the solar arc Sun sextile the Moon (but radical square) in August 1970. One can allow a time orb of several months both ways since both Lights are involved—each with a semi-diameter of 16'! The Moon is radically in the fourth house.

While it need not be so at all, this happens to be an applying Quarter Moon Chart. When such a Sun-Moon square is set off, it frequently refers to a man-woman incompatability, as it does here. The solar arc Pluto reached the conjunction to the Sun in May 1973 and from there moved to the conjunction of the Ascendant in October 1973.

A man was much in evidence in a nonplatonic way (typical of Pluto) in this period. A similar period occurred in which first the Ascendant was trine Uranus and then the Sun did so (by Ascendant arc, of course as the Ascendant may not be moved by solar arc in spite of what Witte may have said). They both set off the radical squares and defined the liberation (Uranus) from her marriage, finalized on January 12, 1971 (on Ascendant to Uranus) with the Sun to Uranus at the beginning of April 1971, thus defining a period of change and radical adjustment. The Ascendant arc Pluto in a square the Midheaven (but radical sextile) of early April 1974 was followed by the ending of a job two months later. The Ascendant conjunction Neptune in July 1966 was followed by her mother's minor surgery in October 1966.

In providing validating aspects of the Lights by direction and of the angles for rectification, I am not giving all of them so as not to be tedious. Unless you can personally deal with the person whose charts you are doing, it is much more difficult, for a list of dates of events never seems to be complete enough. Nor do people always have good memories.

Aspects between charts work, although they are not as powerful. Thus the progressed E Ascendant was square the C Sun in early December 1972, and later that month she terminated an engagement with a man. That C Sun at 9°56′ Aquarius falls in the sixth house of the E Chart in sesquiquadrate to the E Neptune which rules the sign in the seventh house of the E Chart. And the C Sun is square Jupiter and Saturn in the seventh house of the C Chart.

I mention interchart relationships since they are actually a major key to any esoteric astrology. No single chart can reveal more than a certain amount about an individual. Each different chart is a different vantage point from which the individual is viewed. You cannot, for instance, describe all sides of your house from any one vantage point. It is the integration of the various charts that enables us to tell which way the Wheel of Death and Rebirth is revolving (on this, see Alice A. Bailey's *Esoteric Astrology*) or whether that person is living out more than one life during a single physical incarnation.

From Johndro and Brown I learned that one can and should put the C Chart on top of the B Chart, through which it must express, to find out, from their fit how well or poorly the person is able to translate their concepts (C) into actualities (B).

In the end section of this sketchy account I shall introduce the wholly new idea to astrology of postnatal epochs. There are two classes of them: regular and special. The Sun, Moon, and all of the known planets, plus certain others yet to be found have each: a prenatal epoch, a regular postnatal one, and a special postnatal one.

For example, from the Prenatal Epoch of Mars (E of the ego) we are able to time the advent of the special and regular postnatal epochs. For the special ones we take directions and progressions of the Sun of the prenatal chart to its key planet. For the regular postnatal epochs we take directions and progressions of the key planet to the Sun of its prenatal chart.

Thus in the E Chart we move Mars, both directly and conversely, by solar, Ascendant, and vertical arc directions in both longitude and in declination and by secondary progression (directly and conversely in both longitude and declination) to Ptolemaic aspects to the E Sun (conjunction, sextile, square, trine or opposition) or parallels or contraparallels to the E Sun, or E Mars Antiscion or Contrascion E Sun. The quincunx (not a Ptolemaic aspect) may be used to activate a

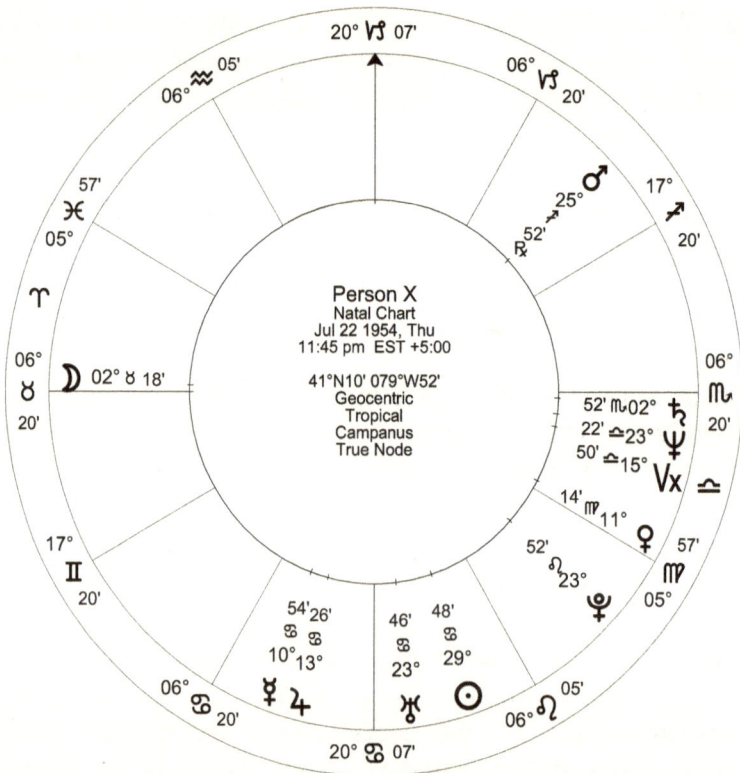

Figure 6, Mars Chart

radical Ptolemaic aspect. The regular postnatal epochs occur in an orbital sequence from Vulcan to Uranus on an average. The epochs of Neptune, Pluto, Isis, Morya, and Lion, which are extra-solar bodies according to *The Mahatma Letters to A.P. Sinnett*, appear to be interspersed among the others with the Pluto and Lion ones in the twenties most often and the other three later.

Any postnatal epoch may occur out-of-sequence, as probably was the case for her early Mars Epoch of Purpose. I once had a client who had his Regular Postnatal Mars Epoch of Purpose at age eight years. I thought that I must have done something wrong. He said that he commenced to save stamps then. He was a stamp dealer who had never really done anything else! So the chart was the correct one. By direct motion the following aspects occurred in her E Chart on E Mars to E Sun:

Mars Trine Sun (arc of 12°27'30")
By solar arc, early July 1954; by Ascendant Arc, November 1956
Mars Square Sun (arc of 42°27'30")
By vertical arc: March 1964
Mars Parallel Sun (declination arc of 4°34')
Solar declination arc, late January 1954; by Ascendant declination arc, start June 1956; by vertical declination arc, March 1971
By Converse Arcs of Direction:
Converse Mars Opposition
Had not yet occurred, and would do so first by vertical arc.

I didn't bother to do the very fast and very early direct vertical arc Mars trine Sun, but would have done so if nothing else worked. Mars would not reach an aspect to the Sun by secondary progression (or by secondary "regression"). It so happens that only one of the above dates can be a Regular Postnatal Mars Epoch.

A Prenatal Solar Epoch, such as the E is, must have its corresponding Regular Postnatal Epoch as a Lunar Epoch, and usually with the Sun about one sign earlier in the zodiac than the prenatal Sun. In like manner, a Prenatal Lunar Epoch has its corresponding Regular Postnatal Epoch as solar, the Sun of that postnatal epoch being about one sign later in the zodiac than the prenatal Sun. Therefore the transiting Sun at the time of the direction that times the year of the chart must be near the area where the Mars Chart's Sun must be, this being the Law of the Sun.

The transiting Moon must be near a conjunction or opposition to the C Ascendant, this being the Law of the Moon that gives the day of the chart. The epoch must occur at moonrise or moonset, which is the Law of the Angles that gives the time of day of the chart. Finally, the usual Law of Sex applies (slightly angular Moon for women and slightly cadent one for men, just as in the F Chart).

Therefore the direction that timed the year of the epoch ought to have occurred in about July, which was only true of the direct solar arc E Mars trine E Sun in early July 1954 when she was a little less than thirteen years of age. Let us imagine a point exactly opposition the C Sun—in this case at 9°56' Leo. If the F Sun is five to thirteen degrees later than this, then the Mars Chart's Sun is likely to be very near the opposition to the C Sun. If, as in the case of X, the F Sun is near or even a little earlier than this point then the Mars Sun will tend to be less than 180° from the C Sun (in the order of the signs).

On July 22, 1954, the Sun was at 29°48' Cancer and thus nearly ten degrees earlier in the zodiac than the point opposition the C Sun. The Moon was at 2°15' Taurus—and thus conjunction the C Ascendant at 0°49'30" Taurus. The Ascendant is at 0°57′ Taurus so that the chart took place at moonrise.

How do we know to use moonrise instead of moonset? If the F Chart is at moonrise, then the Mars Chart is at moonset and vice-versa, as here. Her F Chart occurred at moonset (one reason for doing it before doing this one, although by trial and error we could have determined that this was a moonrise chart). The key planet, Mars, is again in the eighth house, as in the E Chart, but is now retrograde at 25°53′ Sagittarius.

Up until the time of this epoch her father (Saturn) had been extraordinarily strict with her about her relationships (Ascendant) with others—note the seventh house Saturn opposition the Ascendant and also square the fourth house Sun! But the conjunction of Uranus to the Sun in that house showed a quest for freedom that commenced then. More deeply, it accented her roots (Cancer in fourth) and her basic purpose of having her own (Uranus) roots in life. The importance of education, books, and the use of her mind is indicated by Mercury conjunction Jupiter in the third, both opposing the Midheaven C.

She also has Sun/Mars = Mercury/Jupiter, or the midpoint of Sun and the key planet Mars, at 12°55′ Libra, square the midpoint of Mercury and Jupiter at 12°11′ Cancer. This makes this Jupiter-Mercury conjunction quite vital and expansion of the mind becomes a life-purpose. The fixed T-cross of Saturn opposition Ascendant conjunction Moon, all in square to the Sun, is also a dominant configuration, which is indicative of the conflict between security and authority (Saturn rules the Midheaven) on the one hand and the basic drive for having her own independent foundation in life (Uranus).

59

Since the chart seemed probably valid, I skipped the second step and endeavored to rectify it (third step). Vertical arc Pluto came from the fifth house to a trine of the Ascendant about ten days before her marriage—Pluto rules Scorpio in the seventh house. Jupiter rules the eighth and is a co-ruler of the seventh house so that its solar arc square to the Ascendant at the beginning of November 1972 was an index to the broken engagement the next month.

The chart had its angles set on the Ascendant sextile the fourth house Uranus in August 1972, when she moved. The square to Pluto only a month later by the Ascendant may have referred to her emotional problems (Pluto rules the seventh and is in the fifth house) with her fiancee. Her maternal grandfather died on Midheaven opposition Sun in the fourth (the fourth house of the end of things is next in importance to the eighth for deaths) in late September 1967 (the death was two weeks later). In April 1970 the Midheaven was square the Moon, which rules the Cancerian fourth house; her apartment was burglarized that month, on the 27th.

The Midheaven was square the seventh house Saturn in early December 1970 with her divorce final the next month. She ambitiously opened a third house type of store on secondary Jupiter opposition Midheaven in about November 1971, the Midheaven being indicative of this business venture and the Jupiter coming from the third house—a very powerful aspect. The opposition by secondary progression in declination occurred in about August 1973. This may have referred to her late May 1973 move. In any case we have eight aspects that click, and I consider that this is an advisable minimum to be reasonably sure of any rectification.

If anyone wishes to do their Regular Postnatal Neptune Chart, they must take directions and progressions of Neptune in the A Chart to the Sun of that Chart such that the significant aspect hits about a month before the anniversary date of the A Epoch—the transiting Sun should be approximately opposite the B Sun. A leeway of at least a month can be allowed either way. Typically this epoch of surging, as my teacher called it, occurs in the late 30's or early 40's, although it may occur earlier or later.

If the T Chart has its Moon at its Midheaven, which is usual, then the Postnatal Neptune Chart will have its Moon opposition its Midheaven (on the infrequent T Moon opposition its own Midheaven, then Regular Postnatal Neptune Epoch will have its Moon conjunction its own Midheaven). It helps, therefore, to do the T Chart first, although it is not essential. Finally the Neptune Midheaven is nearly the same as the B Midheaven or in opposition to it. I know of no Law as yet which tells us which side of the Midheaven the Moon must be for any chart with the Moon on the upper or the lower Meridian. At a Postnatal Epoch of Surging there is a really major emotional upheaval and someone is often "washed out" of one's life.

The foregoing is merely a succinct preface to prenatal charts since there are still others in the preconceptual period; they all occur on phases of the Moon (New or Full) and have the seven sacred planets as their key planets. They are all covered in my *A Primer of Prenatal and Postnatal Charts*.

Chapter Four

The I̲ Epoch of Inspiration and of Isis and the T̲ Epoch of Ties and of Pluto

The laws of all of the seven prenatal charts within the year before birth will be found in the Appendix at the end of this Section. The Solar I Chart follows the Lunar C Chart. It is followed in turn by the quarter Moon and Lunar T Chart. And that one is then followed by the Solar A Chart. The I Epoch of Isis is like the A Epoch of Neptune in that it is a midnight chart.

Whereas the Epoch of Animation (A) has its Moon conjunction or opposition to the C Midheaven, the Epoch of Inspiration (I) has its Moon conjunction or opposition the B Midheaven. Therefore, one must have a correct B Midheaven in order to do this I Chart. Typically the Sun of the I Chart is seven and one half months or signs of the zodiac before the B Sun. The Law of Sex is the same as for the similar A Epoch.

The native we shall take for our illustrative example was born in 1911 with the natal Sun at 16° Libra. Moving backward in the zodiac, seven and a half signs takes us to early Pisces under the Law of the Sun. Since the natal Midheaven is at 27° Pisces, we look for a day when the Moon will be near that position or opposition to it. This occurred on March 2, 1911. This is the Law of the Moon that gives the day. As already stated, it is a Solar and a Midnight Epoch which thus gives the Law of the Angle and the time of day. Under the Law of Sex the Sun is about a quarter of a degree back from the cusp of the fourth house before the validation and rectification of the chart. It turns out that the chart did not stand up under validation tests.

There are two typical patterns of the Suns of these prenatal charts. There is the predominant nine month case, and the far less common seven month cases. Below I give the idealized positions of the two types with the B Sun at 15°43′ Libra in both cases.

Epoch	9 month	7 month	
U	11 ♏	11 ♏	In the usual 7 month
O	6 ♐	7 ♐ 09	case birth occurs at
C	16 ♑	28 ♑ 35	the E Epoch with the
I	1 ♓	20 ♓	X Epoch of Saturn
T	1 ♈	15 ♈ 43	11 years earlier.
A	16 ♉	11 ♉ 26	This 9 month case
Q	20 ♊	2 ♋ 52	has a typical 7
F	20 ♋	28 ♋ 35	month pattern: Thus
E	11 ♌	24 ♌ 17	his I Chart is two
B	16 ♎	15 ♎ 43	weeks "late."

Nine month cases with seven month patterns are not common but do occur which is why this one is being cited. In the seven month case we draw a seven-sided heptagon. We place the I Sun at its peak—Kether the Grown. One-seventh of circle (a septile of 51°25.7') before the I Sun is the C Sun of Uranus and one-seventh after the I Sun is the A Sun of Neptune—they are a polar pair.

Two-sevenths before the I Sun is the O Sun of the Sun, and two-sevenths after the I Sun is the Q Sun of the Moon—these two are a polar pair. Three-sevenths before the Sun of the I chart is the B Sun, and three-sevenths later than the I Sun is the E Sun, so that Mars and Saturn are paired. The U, T, and F Suns are intermediate between the vertices of the heptagon (25°43') and thus oppose the A, B, and C Suns. In any case our native's I Sun is two weeks later at 23°30' Pisces and the Moon in Virgo instead of in Pisces as it would have been in early March.

The chart is shown in Figure 7 (page 66). It occurred March 15, 1911 at 75W08, 39N54 (geocentric) at 12:11:30 a.m. EST. Isis is shown at 3°53' Aries in the fourth house. Solar arc Saturn opposition the early Sagittarius Ascendant in the late summer of 1944 timed the loss by death of two important people in the last quarter of that year, including his father. The Midheaven contraparallel Pluto late in 1964 timed the onset of his mother's fatal illness that resulted in her death in August 1965.

Under Solar arc Uranus opposition C Midheaven (but radical trine) at the end of 1967 he obtained an excellent job on Wall Street, but lost it suddenly at the end of July 1969 on the Ascendant arc Ascendant conjunction Uranus (radical parallel).

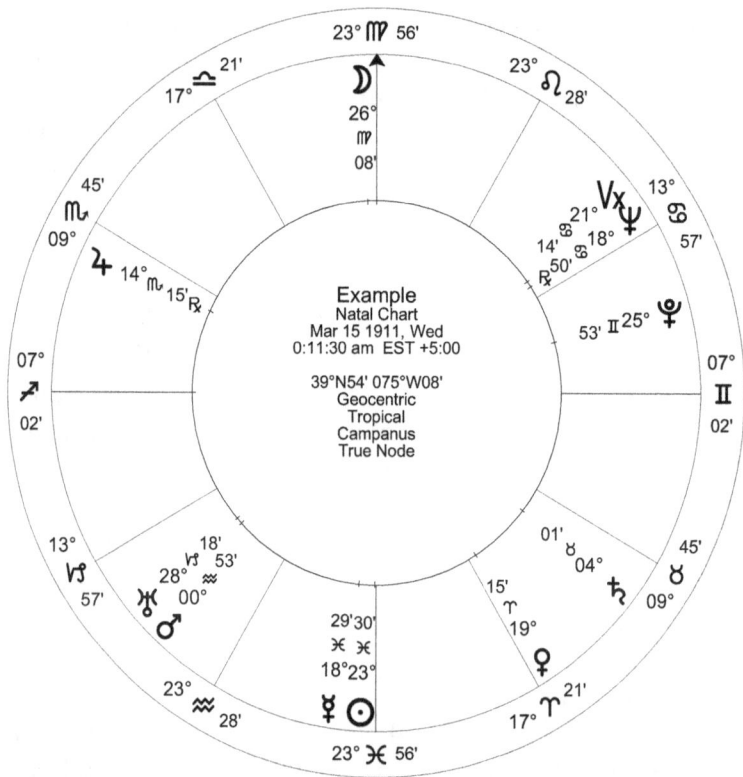

Figure 7

This same progressed Ascendant's opposition to the seventh house Pluto in late 1935, followed in a few months by its square to the Moon, timed a severe psychological crisis in his relationship with an important woman in his life. From January 1972—Midheaven trine Sun to December of that year Sun trine Midheaven—radical opposition in both cases—he experienced major real estate developments with his land.

This chart occurred on a separating Full Moon, although it does not have to do so. The T-cross made by Pluto with the Sun opposition the Moon and Midheaven is the chart's dominant configuration. He has had to cope with many Plutonic types. The conjunction of Neptune to the Vertex, their square to Venus in the fifth house, and their contraparallel to Uranus in the eighth and second houses is another major combination. It fits with the erratic nature of his finances and his tendency to be emotional about such matters. Indeed, the Ascendant is parallel to Uranus and contraparallel to Neptune. In this way the three outermost known planets are configured with all of the three angles and both of the Lights. Such a person is not a conventional type, which is true in this case.

My teacher stated that the I Chart was the "highest" one of the six in the prenatal "set" that are Individual (i.e., do not have to occur on a phase of the Moon). In its higher aspect beyond the "event level" it refers to the Chalice. It is in the Chalice, next to the Heart Center, that the accumulation of the distilled wisdom of all past lives is stored, the brain mechanism being secondary. Thus a careful study of the I Chart can provide valuable clues to the kind of entity that is manifesting in this life. It may be significant that the Isis Cosmic Center, the Galactic Center at about $26°$ Sagittarius, completes the T-cross referred to above. The transiting Sun was crossing this I Chart Midheaven on the day that the native met his teacher.

The example T Chart is shown in Figure 8. Like the Y Chart of Chiron and the O, Q, and F Charts, this T Chart can be done even if the time of birth is unknown. The woman who asked me to rectify her totally unknown birth time was persuaded to let me do her T Chart. She had been born April 24,

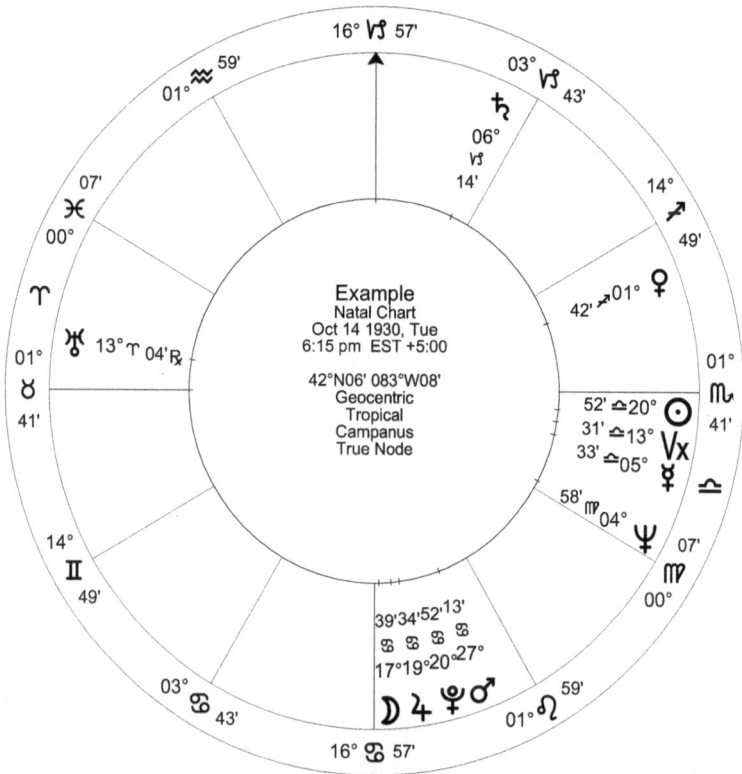

Figure 8

Example
Natal Chart
Oct 14 1930, Tue
6:15 pm EST +5:00

42°N06' 083°W08'
Geocentric
Tropical
Campanus
True Node

16° ♑ 57'

03° ♑ 43'

♄ 06° ♑ 14'

14° ♐ 49'

♀ 42' ♐ 01°

01° ♏ 41'

♃ ♊ 01° ♈ 07'

07° ♓ 00°

♅ 13° ♈ 04' ℞

♉ 01° 41'

52' ♎ 20° ☉

31' ♎ 13° Vx

33' ♎ 05° ☿

♎

58' ♍ 04° ♆

♍ 07' 00°

♊ 14° 49'

39' 34' 52' 13'
♋ ♋ ♋ ♋
17° 19° 20° ♌ 27°

☽ ♃ ♇ ♂

01° ♌ 59'

03° ♋ 43'

16° ♋ 57'

1941 at 83W08, 42N06 (geocentric). With a natal Sun at
about 3°30' Taurus, we go back six and a half signs to find
the T Sun—Law of the Sun. This would place it at about
18°30' Libra. It was found to be at nearly 21° Libra. The
Moon must apply as closely as possible to the square of that
Sun—Law of the Moon. The Moon was at 17°41' Cancer.
The Law of the Angle is that the Moon must be conjunction
or opposition to the Midheaven. Usually it is in conjunction,

but in this case was in opposition to the 17°00′ Capricorn Midheaven. The Law of Sex for lunar epochs with the Moon at the upper or lower Meridian is unknown. One must try the Moon on both sides in rectifying the chart. The epoch occurred at 6:15 p.m. E.S.T. on October 14, 1930.

Since lower culmination Moons in this chart are rare, what conclusions may we draw? In another such case the woman was a medium. In this case the woman was for some years a psychotherapist who used Primal Scream Therapy. She is also very much tuned into the domain of the psychic. The extraordinary thing about this chart is that the key planet, Pluto, is in exact square (less than 1′) to its Sun! Indeed, the chart's pattern is dominated by a loose cardinal grand cross.

All five outer planets except Neptune are part of this grand cross. Mercury, Mars, and the Vertex are also part of it. Neptune is only one degree from the Pluto/Sun midpoint! On solar arc Saturn (father) conjunction the Midheaven and the nearly simultaneous opposition and square of the Sun and Pluto to the Ascendant by solar arc in September 1941, her father went to jail for incestuous relationships with a sister. Mars trine the Ascendant of 1°46′ Taurus (conjunction her B Sun), but radically square, in early 1965 indicated strife with a husband from whom she separated in September of that year. On the Ascendant trine Sun in October 1968 she moved to another city with a man and was happy.

The chart is not shown to demonstrate directions and events. Actually a T Chart, like the A and I, is one of the least overt so ought to be rectified, as Miss Hesseltine maintained, mainly on psychological events. This woman came from a very psychologically difficult family and parental background. Such group charts, as the F̲ and T̲, refer to karmic conditions that the individual must try to transmute, even though those conditions are "shared" with others who have the same group chart! The powerful Pluto here, and the nearby Mars in square to the Ascendant, indicate the strong sexual nature of that which must be transmuted, for they are the two sexual planets.

In her B Chart (that I later rectified from its unknown time) the Leo Mars is square the Taurus Sun, and the Cancer Moon is conjunction Pluto. In 1930, both Jupiter and Pluto near their North Nodes had been aligned with the Sun—a cazimi, which is like an eclipse, so that they were then exceptionally powerful. The grand trine of that ninth house Saturn in Capricorn with the Ascendant and Neptune in Virgo in the sixth house is one of the few resolving factors in this chart. Neptune's parallel to the Ascendant and contraparallel to the Sun make it nearly as potent as her Pluto!

Venus is integrated into the pattern via its square to Neptune, indicative of her irrepressible romanticism. The singleton Uranus as the sole rising planet has an unique importance, especially due to its close opposition to the Vertex. It is this last aspect that decreases the freedom normally shown by a rising singleton Uranus, for the Vertex refers to what we drag after ourselves from our past. Basically the strong cluster at the base of the chart indicates her continuing contact with the contents of the unconscious in a rather primal way.

70

Appendix
Locality Shifts

If any of the prenatal epochs from the C to the E, inclusive, occurs at a locality other than that of birth the following procedure must be followed. One sets the chart up as though it had occurred at the place of birth. Then one shifts the Midheaven to the actual place that the epoch occurred. The simplest way of several to do this is as follows:

Find the Local Mean Time "distance" that the birth place is from Greenwich. Find the same for the actual place of the epoch. The difference between the two is the actual time difference between the two places. In one case the man was born in New York City but conceived in Budapest, Hungary. The time difference was about six hours.

Once his chart had been set up for New York, that time was added to its LMT to find the LMT in Budapest. The Greenwich or Universal Time was of course the same as only the Local Mean Times differed. It put his C Sun at the sunset position which was most suitable as this very brilliant man has translated the works of many people, the accent being on others' (seventh house) ideas (C Chart)!

If the child is a seven month one, then the Moon at the C Epoch will be conjunction or opposition the natal Vertex instead of the natal Ascendant. Johndro did refer to this third angle in the finding of the C Chart in his later work. It may be, therefore, that in seven month gestations the Moon of the U Chart is conjunction or opposition the natal Ascendant instead of the Vertex.

The Laws of the epochs and their horoscopes are shown on page 73.

In sunrise charts, angular and cadent mean that the Sun is about 30' below or above the Ascendant; in midnight epochs it means that if angular, the Sun is about 3° inside the fourth house, but if cadent it means that the Sun is about 15' back from the cusp of that house. The periods in months of the epochs are measured prior to the date of birth and are only the average values, of course.

Type Sym.	Law of Sun	Law of Moon	Law of Angles	Law of Sex Sex	Cosmic Center	Key Planet
S-I U	-11 months	SYZYGY B VX.	Sunrise	Male-Sun Ang. Female-Sun Cad.	15° Virgo	Lion
L-I C	-9 months	SYZYGY B Asc.	Asc. Syz. B Moon	Not Applicable	26° Scorpio	Uranus
S-I I	-7.5 months	SYZYGY B MC	Midnight	Male-Sun Cad. Female-Sun Ang.	26° Sagittarius	Isis
L-G T	-6.5 months	QM Applies	Moon SYZ. OWN MC	Not Applicable	2° Capricorn	Pluto
S-I A	-5 months	SYZYGY C MC	Midnight	Male-Sun Cad. Female-Sun Ang.	Late Aquarius	Neptune
L-G F	-3 months	QM Applies	Moonrise or Set	Male-Moon Cad. Female-Moon Ang.	26° Aries	Morya
S-I E	-2 months	SYZYGY C VX.	Sunrise	Male-Sun Ang. Female-Sun Cad.	0° Gemini	Mars
L-I B	-0 months	SYZYGY C Asc.	Asc. Syz. C Moon	Not Applicable	7° Leo	Saturn

Abbreviations: S, Solar; L, Lunar; I, Individual Epoch; G, Group (lunar phase) Epoch; SYZYGY or Syz., conjunction or opposition

www.ingramcontent.com/pod-product-compliance
Lightning Source LLC
LaVergne TN
LVHW011411080426
835511LV00005B/486